I0411323

134 Ways to Become a Fantastic Trainer

Tips for understanding clients' wants and needs

Gail Cassidy

Copyright © 2013 by Gail Cassidy. All rights reserved.
This book or any portion thereof may not be reproduced or
used in any manner whatsoever without the express written
permission of the publisher except for the use of brief
quotations in a book review.
Disclaimer and Terms of Use:
The Author and Publisher has strived to be as accurate and
complete as possible in the creation of this book,
notwithstanding the fact that he does not warrant or
represent at any time that the contents within are accurate
due to the rapidly changing nature of the Internet. While all
attempts have been made to verify information provided in
this publication, the Author and Publisher assume no
responsibility for errors, omissions, or contrary interpretation
of the subject matter herein. Any perceived slights of specific
persons, peoples, or organizations are unintentional.

Printed in the United States of America, First Printing.

Tomlyn Publications
547 Shackamaxon Drive
Westfield, NJ 07090
http://www.coachability.com
gail@coachability.com

DEDICATION

Whether you are a trainer who coaches athletes, racehorses, or show animals, I dedicate this book to you—for your patience, your dedication, your knowledge, and your positive effect on others. You are making a difference!

134 Ways to Become a Fantastic Trainer

Tips for understanding clients' wants and needs

Table of Contents

TIPS FOR TRAINERS

Motivational words and phrases can be the reminders a trainer and/or a client may need to keep them going. *Chris Freytag, Fitness Expert for Prevention Magazine & ACE Board Member* said, "I am addicted to motivational words and phrases. I have them on my laptop screen saver and on my iPhone. I wear a necklace that says "Live Life Well". I have bracelets with coins saying "Believe, Sweat, and Inspire". I get energy from words. I glance at them, read them, repeat them and they channel my thoughts in a positive way. It's a great way to keep you motivated with your fitness program. It can be as simple as putting the word or phrase on a post-it note on your computer or bathroom mirror – somewhere you will see it every day."

Hopefully, trainers will be able to find inspiration and motivation on the following pages. Communication skills, attitude, and human relation skills are important to master in order to be the best trainer he or she can be.

Being a trainer is such a wonderful and satisfying profession, but it is also one that can be filled with challenges and frustrations. From my many years of public/private school and corporate training, I have found the following tips to be relevant for all training situations, no matter what the age of the participant or the topic being taught.

Enjoy reading the tips. Highlight those you want to keep in the forefront of your mind. Enjoy every trainee you work with. Each one will give you far more than you will give to them. Their unique ideas, their individual perspectives, and their humor will provide you with the gift of never-ending fond memories. Best of all, they will be healthier because of you!

ENJOY!
Gail Cassidy

PHILOSOPHY

1. See the invisible tattoo on everyone's forehead that reads: **"PLEASE MAKE ME FEEL IMPORTANT."**

2. Find at least one happening in each training session to be grateful for.

3. Look for positives in every participant.

4. Recognize the specialness of diversity.

5. Provide an atmosphere conducive to learning e.g. posters, adages, lighting, safety, etc.

6. Vary your training activities. Do something different that they will remember.

7. Remember, humans of any age cannot listen and absorb for extended periods of time-20-25 minutes maximum/break/continue.

8. Get participants involved with teaching. Everyone has something special to offer.

9. Becoming the teacher is when you learn. -Covey

10. Learn the Serenity Prayer: "God, grant me the serenity to accept the things I cannot change, courage to

change the things I can and the wisdom to know the difference."

11. "See" and/or "feel" your positive training situation before the class starts via positive self-talk.

12. Be (or act) enthusiastic about everything you do. It's contagious; it carries over to the participants.

13. Accept participants as they are, and then provide the atmosphere for them to learn and love learning.

14. Learn from every colleague, every trainee.

15. Ask yourself, "Does it really matter?"

16. Being right does not always work, e.g.,

Here lies the body of William Jay,
Who died maintaining his right of way.
He was right, dead right as he sped along,
But he's just as dead as if he were wrong.

17. **HAVE FUN!**

ATTITUDE

18. Park your ego at the door; it hinders relationships with trainees.

19. Give trainees a reason to check their negative attitudes at the door also.

20. Know that trainees "mirror" you. They reflect what they see, hear, and feel from you.

21. Shake things up. Make changes. "If you always do what you have always done, you'll always get what you've always got."

22. Show participants through your own example what fun having a great attitude is.

23. Be patient.

24. Positive attitudes in class are catching.

25. Show respect to get respect.

26. Know that attitude is a choice everyone makes every day.

27. Explain that people cannot help what happens to them, but they are always in charge of their responses.

28. Remember, there is a pause between stimulus and response. Choose your response carefully.

29. Ask your clients why they are choosing to be unhappy, bored, tired, sad, happy.

30. Know that attitude is the steering mechanism of the brain. Body language can lead to attitude.

31. Have trainees practice changing their attitudes by sitting or standing straight, with their heads up, and a smile on their faces. It does work!

32. Know that it is the attitude of our hearts and minds that shape who we are, how we live, and how we treat others.

33. Help trainees to recognize their specialness.

34. Success is feeling good about yourself every single day. That is attitude.

35. Know and share with your participants that true power is knowing that you can control your attitude at all times.

HUMAN RELATIONS

36. Treat every trainee as if he or she were your friend's best friend.

37. Never talk down to anyone.

38. Find what is special about every participant.

39. **SMILE.** It warms a training room.

40. Use tact when responding to a challenging participant. The rewards outweigh "being right."

41. Know that it is not okay for any trainee or client to feel your negativity.

42. Be 100% fair at all times--no exceptions.

43. Keep in mind that perception is reality--yours and your trainees.

44. Treat every person as you wish to be treated.

45. Understand that no one wants to be wrong.

46. Everyone desperately wants to feel special.

47. Remember that people gravitate toward things that are pleasurable and avoid things that are painful. Make learning pleasurable.

48. **LISTENING** is the greatest compliment.

49. Try to understand before being understood.

50. Show genuine appreciation to participants.

51. Begin corrective action with sincere and honest recognition of what has been done correctly.

52. Never embarrass a trainee. Allow the person to save face.

53. Use encouragement. Make the error seem easy to correct.

54. Don't be afraid to admit your mistakes. It will make you appear more human to students.

55. Show respect for every trainee's opinion.

56. Challenge clients to be the best that they can be.

57. Make **SINCERITY** your No. 1 priority.

COMMUNICATION

58. Set standards in your training room and share them with your trainees.

59. Explain the purpose and importance of what you are teaching. Give them a reason why they should learn the material. Personalize it.

60. Set high expectations. There is a true story about the new teacher who thought the locker list from 140-160 was the list of IQ's in her class. She treated them accordingly, and they performed accordingly.

61. Know that 55% of all messages comes from the body. Notice how you can tell your special someone is in a bad mood without any words being spoken.

62. Know that 38% of the message comes from the voice: inflection, intonation, pitch, speed, e.g., "I didn't say he stole the exam." Seven words = seven meanings.

63. Know that you cannot **NOT** communicate.

64. Recognize that we don't all see the same thing when looking at the same thing.

65. Know also that we don't all hear the same things even when listening to the same words.

66. Control your thoughts; your feelings come from your thoughts; therefore, you can also control your feelings! Choice is control.

67. Teach participants to take responsibility for what they say and how they say it.

68. Listen for the message, yet know that body language can be interpreted as only a clue to the meaning of the message, e.g., arms crossed in front of chest could mean blocking you or could mean person is actually cold or comfortable.

69. Learn to lead rather than to try and overcome resistance.

70. Communicate your enthusiasm through your body and voice.

71. "One who is too insistent on his own views, find few to agree with him." -Lao-Tze

72. Speak with a warm heart.

SELF ESTEEM

73. Know that a person with high self-esteem does not need to find fault with others.

74. Remind trainees that people find fault with others when they feel threatened, consciously or unconsciously.

75. Know that self-esteem is not noisy conceit. It is a quiet sense of self-respect, a feeling of self-worth. Conceit is whitewash to cover low self-esteem.

76. Remember, people have two basic needs: to know they are lovable and worthwhile.

77. Remember, it is the participant's feeling about being respected or not respected that affects how s/he will behave and perform.

78. Helping clients build their self-concept is the key to successful training.

79. Know that your words have power to affect a trainee's self-esteem.

80. Each participant values himself to the degree s/he has been valued.

81. Words are less important in their affect on self-esteem than the judgments that accompany them.

82. The attitude of others toward a participant's capacities is more important than his possession of particular traits.

83. Bragging people are asking for positive reflections.

84. Masks are worn to hide the "worthless me."

85. Low self-esteem is tied to impossible demands on the self.

86. A trainer's own self-acceptance frees him or her to focus on the trainee, unencumbered by inner needs.

87. The single most important ingredient in a nurturing relationship is honesty.

88. Ask this: "If I were to treat my friends as I treat my clients/trainees, how many friends would I have left?"

89. Avoid mixed messages. Be clear in your statements of expectations.

DISCIPLINE

90. Tolerate no disrespect.

91. Be consistent in enforcing rules.

92. Set boundaries.

93. Find opportunities for each trainee to improve the quality of his/her work.

94. Differentiate between the action and the person.

95. Uncover and address, when possible, the reasons for the trainees poor performance.

96. Make sure participants have the skills to succeed.

97. Focus, as often as possible, on what is right rather than what is wrong.

98. Give plenty of recognition for the unique gifts of each trainee.

99. Teach trainees to know they have power in the present moment to change their thoughts, feelings, and attitude about the past.

100. Remind participants to take control of their lives by focusing on the present.

101. Remove the word "try" from trainees' vocabulary. Have them "try" to pick up a pencil. Either they do or they don't.

102. Work with clients to find the lesson or value in unacceptable situations.

103. Make sure participants know they have choices in spite of their past experiences.

104. Set an example by turning any problem into a learning opportunity.

105. Make sure assignments are clear to every trainee.

106. Approach problematic trainees with relaxed confidence.

107. Being a model for trainees to follow provides them with a picture of what appropriate behavior looks like.

108. Respond thoughtfully to challenging and/or problem situations--avoid making judgments.

109. Teach problem solving:

   o   State the problem
   o   Look for causes of the problem
   o   Brainstorm solutions
   o   Choose the best one

110. Patience is the companion of wisdom. -Augustine

111. Encourage habits of thought conducive to growth in understanding others, to think outside the box.

112. Recognize that there is no one interpretation of text.

113. Strive for progress, not perfection. -Unknown

114. Know that you too are special.

115. Enjoy each day and each trainee.

116. Make corrections by citing two positives for every negative.

117. Make learning relevant to the participants' lives.

118. Be alert to teachable moments.

119. Show lively enthusiasm!

120. Create an atmosphere of fun.

121. Build on successes.

122. Create a routine with varied activities.

123. Turn participants on to learning.

124. Encourage trainees to visualize doing well.

125. Have a relaxed training room.

126. Make every trainee feel important.

127. Give one instruction at a time.

128. Give participants opportunities to succeed.

129. Provide a safe atmosphere.

130. Validate participants frequently.

131. Understand participants' learning modalities, e.g., visual, kinesthetic, auditory.

132. Recognize the positive value of peer pressure in learning, no matter what the ages of the group.

133. Recognize that everyone is on a quest for identity and some sense of personal power.

134. Above all, enjoy each day--your participants will also. You are the mirror.

TIPS FOR MANAGEMENT

- Validate your trainers on a regular basis, not just during a once-a-year review.

- Tell trainers specifically what you like about what they are doing. They will work harder to earn that recognition again in the future.

- Encourage trainers to strive for excellence. "We are what we repeatedly do. Excellence, then, is not an act but a habit." -Aristotle.

- Encourage trainers to align their goals with their values. Conflict arises when the two are in conflict.

- Expect the best from your staff. People live up to expectations.

- Always abide by the golden rule: "Do unto others as you would have them do unto you."

- Involve as many trainers as you can in company/corporate activities. Those who participant feel more a part of the "family."

- Always always be fair.

- Avoid being judgmental.

- Treat your trainers to a special treat once in a while. Let them know you care.

- Encourage trainers to use their powers of observation and logic. Successful trainers see details and discover principles that others do not.

- Encourage and enable trainers to continually grow. Complacency breeds stagnation.

- Make your company/corporation an inviting place to work.

- Make your trainers proud to be a part of your "family."

TIPS FOR ALL STAFF

- Work towards feeling good about yourself. It is man's highest goal.

- Always do what you feel is right or true.

- Your actions reveal your values.

- Your thought is the most powerful force in your universe. "Nothing is either good or bad but thinking makes it so." -Shakespeare.

- Whatever you dwell on expands.

- Work toward goals that cause you to feel a sense of mastery.

- Write a list of everything you have accomplished or have been recognized for in your life. Add to it whenever you think of something new. Read it when the going gets tough.

- Have a clear sense of purpose in life.

- Clarify your goals and focus on them

- Be a risk taker. Step outside your comfort zone. Try something new.

- Polish your people skills.

- Hone your communications skills.

- Take excellent care of yourself.

- Positive expectations are the single, most outwardly identifiable, characteristics all successful people possess.

- Your reality is what you make it to be.

- You can train yourself to think more positively by training yourself to choose what you pay attention to and what you say about it, both to yourself and others. "We know what we are but know not what we may be." -Shakespeare.

- Whatever you believe, picture in your mind, and think about most of the time, you eventually will bring into reality.

- Your self-image is the most dominant factor that affects everything you attempt to do.

- Nothing is more exciting than the realization that you can accomplish anything you really want that is consistent with your unique mix of natural talents and abilities.

WORTHY QUOTES

- Assume a virtue, if you have it not. - Shakespeare.

- Act enthusiastic and you'll be enthusiastic. -Carnegie.

- Begin to be now what you will be hereafter. - St. Jerome.

- Repetition is the mother of skill.

- It is not the place, nor the condition, but the mind alone that can make any one happy or miserable. - L Estrange.

- Beliefs have the power to create and the power to destroy. -Robbins.

- Nothing is more likely to help a person overcome or endure troubles than the consciousness of having a task in life. -Frankl.

- When the student is ready, the teacher will appear. - Zen proverb.

- The ancestor to every action is a thought. -Emerson.

- Imagination is more important than knowledge. -Albert Einstein.

- Train so that you won't be ashamed to sell the training room parrot to the town gossip. - Will Rogers, adapted.

- Teaching does not make a teacher; it reveals him. - James Allen, adapted.

- Things do not change; we change. -Thoreau.

- Change your thoughts and you change your world. - Norman Vincent Peale.

- Great men are those who see that thoughts rule the world. -Emerson.

- Nothing has any power over me other than that which I give it through my conscious thoughts. -Anthony Robbins.

- The greatest discovery of my generation is that human beings can alter their lives by altering their attitudes of mind. -William James.

- You are what you choose today. -Dyer.

- I am indebted to my father for living, but to my trainer for living well. -Alexander of Macedon.

- The highest function of the teacher consists not so much in imparting knowledge as in stimulating the pupil in its love and pursuit. - Amiel.

- The one exclusive sign of a thorough knowledge is the power of teaching. - Aristotle.

- The teacher who is attempting to teach without inspiring the pupil with a desire to learn is hammering on cold iron. -H. Mann.

- The best teacher is the one who suggests rather than dogmatizes, and inspires his listener with the wish to teach himself. -Bulwer.

- To waken interest and kindle enthusiasm is the sure way to teach easily and successfully. -Tyron Edwards.

- The most potent of all indirect influences in the development of our citizenry is the influence of a good teacher. -Armand J. Gerson.

- The only limits you have are the limits you believe. -Wayne Dyer.

- Anything we fail to reinforce will eventually dissipate. -Robbins.

- Teaching is not a lost art, but the regard for it is a lost tradition. -Newsweek.

- Teachers believe they have a gift for giving; it drives them with the same irrepressible drive that drives others to create a work of art or a market or a building. -Bartlett Giamatti.

- The more he gives to others, the more he possesses of his own. -Lao-Tze.

- Vision is the art of seeing things invisible. -Swift.

- What the mind can conceive and believe, it can achieve. -Hill.

- Believing is seeing. -Dyer.

- Nothing in the world can take the place of persistence. Talent will not; nothing is more common than unsuccessful men with talent. Genius will not; un-rewarded genius is almost a proverb. Education will not; the world is full of educated derelicts. Persistence and determination alone are omnipotent. -Calvin Coolidge

- Your persistence is your belief in yourself. -Brian Tracy

- Focus on the value of what you have to give, not on your weakness, and act. - Anonymous

- Thousands of people have talent... The one and only thing that counts is: Do you have staying power? - Anonymous

- Persistence prevails when all else fails. -Anonymous

- Life always gets harder toward the summit; the cold increases, the responsibility increases. -Friedrich Nietzsche

- If one advances confidently in the direction of their

dreams, and endeavors to lead a life which they have imagined they will meet with a success unexpected in common hours. -Henry David Thoreau

- The great end of life is not knowledge, but action. - Aldous Huxley

- It doesn't happen all at once ... You become. It takes a long time. -Margery Williams

- Do what you can with what you have, where you are. - Theodore Roosevelt

- Our aspirations are our possibilities. -Robert Browning

- Always bear in mind that your own resolution to succeed is more important than any other one thing. - Abraham Lincoln

- He conquers who endures. -Persius

- A strong passion ... will insure success, for the desire of the end will point out the means. -William Hazlitt

- Act as though it were impossible to fail. -Winston Churchill

- No one can be the best in everything, but you can be your best in everything you do. -Dave Bruno

- The difference between the possible an the impossible lies in a man's determination. -Tommy Lasorda

- Nothing is particularly hard if you divide it into small jobs. -Henry Ford

- The quality of a person's life is in direct proportion to their commitment to excellence regardless of their chosen field of endeavor. -Vince Lombardi

- Trifles make perfection and perfection is no trifle. -Michelangelo

- Spectacular achievements are always preceded by unspectacular preparation. -Roger Staubach

- Life is a fight. You must remain concentrated and not reveal your defects; through continuous training and self-control, gradually you discard them. -Taisen Deshimaru

- If people knew how hard I worked to get my mastery, it wouldn't seem so wonderful after all. -Michelangelo

- I want to be thoroughly used up when I die, for the harder I work the more I live. I rejoice in life for its own sake. -George Bernard Shaw

- You are what you do. - Anonymous

- A journey of a thousand miles is many thousand steps. -Anonymous

- Great works are performed not be strength, but by perseverance. -Samuel Johnson

- The best preparation for good work tomorrow is to do good work today. -Elbert Hubbard

- Never give in, never give in, never, never, never, never... -Winston Churchill

- Those who reach greatness on earth reach it through concentration. -Upanishads

- There is nothing with which every man is so afraid as getting to know how enormously much he is capable of doing and becoming. -Soren Kierkegaard

- Keep away from people who try to belittle your ambitions. Small people always do that, but the really great make you feel that you, too, can become great.

-Mark Twain

- You must be the change you wish to see in the world. -Mahalma Gandi

- Attitudes are more important than facts. -Carl Menninger

http://www.la-personal-trainer.com/motivationalquotes.htm

TEN WAYS TO ENHANCE TRAINING IN YOUR ORGANIZATION

GOALS: Create community through the sharing of ideas; develop leadership; promote excellence, and prepare trainees to the best of their abilities.

1. Give each trainer a copy of 134 Ways to Become a Fantastic Trainer.

2. Personalize the booklets with your company logo.

3. Have copies available for participants.

4. Give booklet to each new prospective client.

5. Use for discussion with staff members.

6. Encourage trainers to use these concepts for research.

7. Ask trainers to add to the lists.

8. Use individual lists as topics for general discussion. Find out where there is agreement and where there is not.

9. Use these principles as the basis for your organization's standards.

10. Study the various lists and add new points and new topics. This will be an opportunity to expand the consciousness of trainers and bosses.

Teachers (trainers) affect eternity; they can never tell where their influence stops.
-Henry Adams

For information on how to personalize copies of this Tips book for your organization, please contact gail@coachability.com.

www.ingramcontent.com/pod-product-compliance
Lightning Source LLC
Chambersburg PA
CBHW070514290526
45790CB00003B/1234